MW00814770

"Son" Flower
BLESSINGS

God's miracles are all around us.
We just need to open our eyes.

ISBN 978-1-0980-7237-7 (paperback)
ISBN 978-1-0980-7238-4 (digital)

....tian Faith Publishing, Inc.

them all over the
....tand tall

Acknowledgment

I dedicate this book to my wonderful husband, Reverend Ed Rogers, who went home to Jesus on February 20, 2019. We were married for forty-eight and a half years, not nearly enough time on this earth. I always said that we packed ninety years of life into the forty-eight years we were married. Ed was a unique human being and one of the smartest men I knew. We raised a family of six children: Marsha, Dawn, Tom, Tim, Jeff, and Susie. He loved his grandchildren with a passion. Heidi was his first, and he encouraged her every day. He even taught her to drive. Kassi was his beautiful mechanic and loved to work on cars. Cole was his only grandson, and he taught him so much about tools and fixing things (even at eight, Cole could fix a lawnmower). Tori was his sunshine; she is always singing about Jesus and brighten every room she comes into. Emmy was his youngest, and she could come up with the most surprising answers and did it with drama.

Before Ed died with leukemia, he called each grandchild and talked to them about heaven and that he would be leaving this earth soon. He told them not to be mad at God but to serve and love Jesus with all their heart. Ed was an awesome pastor and loved all the people he pastored. He prayed for them, held funerals, dedicated babies, and visited the sick. He was the hands and feet and heart of Christ. Ed, I miss you so much, but I chose joy for the years we had together, and I know that we will be together again one day. While I am left on this earth for a season, I will try to continue the work in the life centers we started. Jesus is a life giver!

Jesus, Mama, and the Sunflowers

Whoever listens to me will dwell safely,
And will be secure, without fear of evil.
—Proverbs 1:33 NKJV

My daddy was an awesome man of God. He was a World War II veteran and served in the Navy. He loved farming and talked about feeling close to God on the tractor. Daddy's last years were hard; he had to have a feeding tube. He was bedridden with Parkinson's. No matter how hard the days, he would always brighten up when you talked about Jesus. One night he had to be put in the hospital. During the night, he died, but God sent him back. The next morning, I asked Daddy what he had seen during his near-death experience. He smiled and said, "I saw your mama and Jesus at the end of a road. It was beautiful. The road had big beautiful sunflowers down each side." I smiled. You see, I love sunflowers. They remind me of God's love. They are beautiful and follow the sun and are filled with lots of seeds. Just like us, we should follow the son and share the seeds of God's Word. I thanked God for Daddy's vision. You see, I knew that Jesus and Mama were in heaven. I was delighted to know that God loves sunflowers too.

Jeremiah

Let us therefore come boldly to the throne
of grace, that we may obtain mercy and
find grace to help in time of need.
—Hebrews 4:16 NKJV

I am the director of a crisis pregnancy center. I receive many calls each week from mothers who need help. A client named Kay (not her real name) called, and she was in trouble and in deep depression. I had met Kay about fifteen months before. She had gone to an abortion clinic, and one of the Christians who was praying in front of the abortion directed her across the street to the pregnancy center. She already had three children and has accepted Christ four years prior. She had promised God that she would wait on sex and marry. A young man came along with lots of sweet talk and lots of promises that would be broken after he got what he wanted. As a Christian, she knew that she should not abort, but there were so many burdens in her life already. We talked, and she left the center undecided on what she would do with the baby.

Later on, she called to say that she was going to keep the baby. Little Jeremiah was born in the summer. He was so handsome, and she felt that she had made a good choice. God had saved Jeremiah from an abortion. This call came ten months later. She said she couldn't take care of Jeremiah anymore. She felt that the baby looked too much like his father. Kay was in depression, and I was concerned for the baby. We went and picked up the baby and brought him home with us. Kay gave us temporary custody of Jeremiah. She was going to the doctor to get help.

Jeremiah was ten months old and had the biggest smile with two teeth. We all fell in love with him. On the way home, he started to cry. The whole family started singing "Jesus Loves Me" and other Jesus songs. He smiled and finally went to sleep. I wept as I watched my husband, my daughters, and my grandchildren love on Jeremiah. I never heard my grandchildren say, "Gega, do you know that Jeremiah is different?" Love is color blind. I started to pray that God would heal his mom and turn her heart to Jeremiah. I called other prayer warriors. God whispered in my ear and said, *Write a letter to Kay from Jeremiah*. God gave me the words. Here is the letter:

Dear Mom,

Thank you for giving me life. I know it is hard, but I love you. Next to God, you are the most important person in my life. You said it is hard to look at me because I look like my earthly father, but please remember that I was created in the image of my Heavenly Father. God did not make a mistake by giving you to me as my *mom*. He chose you for me. He knows you will teach me about God and His ways. He will walk with you as you raise me, and when I am grown, I will be a mighty man of God. You know that the name *Jeremiah* means "God will lay the foundation for Christ." You will be proud of me. Mom, I will take care of you when you are old. I love my brother and sisters. I know that you have to do what is right for the family, and if that means adopting me to a kind, loving family, I will understand and love you. Mom, there are people praying for you. God has not forsaken you nor forgotten you. He died on the cross for you and me. You have accepted Jesus, and He has forgiven you. Please know that God has plans for me and for you. Miss Helen said to read Psalm 91, and you will find the answers you need.

Love,
Your son Jeremiah

Kay called and had gotten some help from her doctor. We took Jeremiah home. The whole family is doing better. We miss Jeremiah; my family wept when he left. I am so thankful for my family; they cared for and loved a little stranger that God sent into our lives. God really has plans for Jeremiah; his life has been saved two times. He was saved from an abortion and from a depressed mom. What will we do to help save a life? Whatever it takes! Children are gifts from God.

The Diaper

She extends her hand to the poor, Yes, she
reached out her hands to the needy.
—Proverbs 31:20 NKJV

Tori is one of my precious granddaughters. When she was two, I stopped by to see her. I was on the way to the crisis pregnancy center. I stayed awhile and started to leave. She asked me to stay with her. I told her that I had to go to the center to help moms and babies. I shared with her that we gave clothes and diapers to new babies who didn't have any. Tori was thoughtful for a minute, and then she said, "Babies need diapers." She went over to her pack of pull-ups and gave me a diaper for the babies. Tori said, "Gega, this is for the babies. They need it more than me. I love babies." Do you love babies enough to share what the Lord has blessed you with? The Bible says that a child shall lead them. Let's follow their lead.

Tree Money

The Lord is My Shepherd; I shall not want.
—Psalm 23:1 NKJV

The Agape PSS had some trees on the property that were causing damage to the roof. We needed $2,000 to have the trees removed. Someone gave me $7 for the tree removal. I thanked God for the $7 and for the rest of the $2,000. A soldier came by and told me God had told him to give me this precise donation. I opened the envelope, and the check was for $1993.06. God always answers prayers. I am so thankful that the soldier listened to God. We got the trees cut, and we know that God sent it.

Late Bloomer

For with God nothing will be impossible.
—Luke 1:37 NKJV

I had a young woman to come to the pregnancy center the other day. Sarah said, "I just came back by to thank you. You helped me when I was sixteen years old. I wanted to abort my baby, but you helped me. I had the baby, and she is fourteen years old now. I still did not listen to you about needing Jesus. I had five abortions, and last month, I got saved. My life has changed radically. What you said was true." Sometimes we do not realize that some seeds bloom later than others. It took fourteen years for the seeds of truth to reach her heart. Now she is telling her story so that others will come to know Jesus. Christians need to continue to share the Good News with everyone they meet.

Flood Relief

In the day when I cried out, You answered me,
And made me bold with strength in my soul.
—Psalm 138:3 NKJV

I am blessed with my precious grandchildren. Not too long ago, a hurricane flooded parts of Louisiana. My granddaughter Heidi was sad and wanted to help the people in Louisiana. She looked up the crisis pregnancy centers in that area. She found one that had lost everything. They lost all their ultrasound machines, baby items, and education materials. She asked me if we could collect baby items to take to Louisiana to the center in need. We let the Christian community know about the mission. We collected baby items for a month and loaded the items into a truck and delivered them to the center in Louisiana. The number of items collected was over $10,000 worth. The center director was so happy to receive the baby items, for the needs were great because of the flood. Heidi learned early that you can be a missionary no matter how young you are. There are needs all around us, and we should all be missionaries. Take a look around. You are called by our Heavenly Father to be the difference.

I'm Used to It

So, after he had patiently endured,
he obtained the promise.
—Hebrews 6:15 NKJV

My granddaughter Tori is a bundle of joy. She is stubborn and very strong-willed. Cole is her five-year-old brother. He looks after her. One day Tori turned over a little rocking chair, and it fell on Cole's leg. She sat down on the chair with Cole's leg under the chair. I told Tori she was hurting Cole and to get up so she wouldn't hurt her brother. Cole looked at me and said, "Gega, it is okay. I am used to it." How many times are we hurt by someone we love? We overlook the pain because we love them. How many times has God overlooked the times that we have hurt him because of our sin? He is still so in love with us. Love is God's language.

Hurricane Matthew

When you pass through the waters,
I will be with you; And through the
rivers, they shall not overflow you.
—Isaiah 43:2 NKJV

Hurricane Matthew was a disaster for North Carolina. There was so much flooding. I have a friend who lived in Lumberton. Lumberton got the full force of the flooding. I called her after the hurricane and asked how she was. She told me that they had lost their home, and even the elementary school she was a teacher at had been destroyed. Then she said, "We are good. We still have everything. We still have our faith in God, and our family is safe." It took them a year to get a new home. If we lose all our physical possessions, can we still say, "I have everything, I have Jesus"?

Restored

A man's heart plans his way, But
the Lord directs his steps.
—Proverbs 16:9 NKJV

I have a friend who volunteers at the pregnancy center. Last year she was pregnant, and her beautiful baby girl died. Her heart was broken. She loves the Lord, and she grieved her baby. A year later, she wanted to do something special in memory of her little girl. She had a baby shower for the pregnancy center in memory of her precious baby. Just before she went to the shower for the center, she took a pregnancy test and found out she was expecting. She said God had sent a rainbow after the storm. God loves us so much, and He has promised that He would restore the years that the locusts have eaten. We all have those locust times. If we continue to love and serve Jesus, He keeps all His promises.

Big Undies

I had to speak at a women's conference one year. I did a skit about a mom trying to get ready for a women's conference and all the preparation she had to do for her trip. Examples included laying out the clothes for the three children for the two days mom would be gone, preparing food and putting it in storage containers in the refrigerator, labeled. If mom didn't do these things, dad would forget to feed the kids. I even used the illustration that I personally had to make sure my three pairs of underwear were clean. The ladies all laughed and completely understood about all the preparations. That evening, the ladies presented me with a huge pair of size 64 underwear as a joke. We all laughed. Life is what we make it. Live life to the fullest, laugh often, and love the Lord with all your heart.

Tori the Tiger Calls Papa

This is the day that the Lord has made;
we will rejoice and be glad in it.
                                        —Psalm 118:24 NKJV

Tori was three years old, and she loved tigers. I came to visit one day, and I asked Tori, "How's my little princess today?" She looked at me and said, "Gega, I not a princess. I a tiger—*grrrrr*." How many times do we want to change our identity? God has made us special; there is no one like us in the world. We are one of a kind made by the Great Creator. Tori is also the granddaughter who loves her Papa Ed.

One day I was babysitting her, and I asked Tori if she wanted to call Papa Ed. She went over to the door, and as loud as she could, she called, "Papa Ed!" I laughed. How many times do we do that to our Heavenly Father? We don't have to call our Abba Daddy on a telephone. We can just call His name. God is always near to us.

Thank You, Lord, for the Leaking Roof

For with God nothing is impossible.
—Luke 1:37 NKJV

Hurricane Matthew came through and damaged our roof on the pregnancy center building. There were twenty leaks all through the building, and every time it rained, we had to put buckets under the leaks. Some of the babies' clothes got damaged, and there were lots of ceiling damage and mold. I called to find out how much it would cost to fix our roof. The cost was $18,200. That was an impossible amount for us. Our small ministry did not have that kind of money. I prayed, and I didn't know how to get this amount; it would have to be God. I cried out to God, and He said, *Let My children know.*

I called a friend at a home church and asked if his church could help. They planned a BBQ sale for us. All this time, it was still raining in the center. I sent out newsletters and asked for help with the repair. God's people responded. We collected $70,000. This amount fixed our roof, did the repairs inside, paid off the mortgage on the building, paid off the center van, and let us buy a used RV to create a mobile crisis center. What was an awful thing turned into a wonderful blessing! I always say that God can take stinking rotten situations and turn them into a garden of flowers. We serve a mighty God, and there is nothing too hard for my Jesus.

There may be some rotten things in your life right now. God is fixing to use it for fertilizer and turn it into a flower garden.

The Speaker Has Laryngitis

Submit to God-Resist the devil and he will
flee from you. Humble yourself in the sight
of the Lord and He will lift you up.
—James 4:7 NKJV

I speak in a lot of churches about the pregnancy ministry. On Sunday, I got up and started getting ready for church and had laryngitis. No sound would come from my mouth. I prayed and asked God to bless this day and my voice. I went to the church, and I met the pastor at the door. I wrote him a note. He told me we could cancel and do it another day. I told him God had a plan for this, and I wanted everything to go on as planned. I said that God would have the glory for what He was going to do. He looked worried. He introduced me and told everyone that I had laryngitis and to pray for me. I got up, whispered a prayer, and opened my mouth. I shared about the pregnancy ministry for thirty minutes, telling of the goodness of God. I prayed and said amen and sat down. The pastor said it was truly a miracle. As I left the church that day, my laryngitis returned. God gave me what I needed. God is always a God on time. The enemy did not want the pregnancy center story told, but God did.

What is the enemy trying to keep you from doing for Jesus? Submit to God and call out to Jesus, and the devil will flee from you. He can't stay around if Jesus is there.

The Love Flowers

The heavens declare the glory of God; And
the firmament shows His handiwork.
—Psalm 19:1 NKJV

Adults see dandelions as weeds and as a nuisance in the yard. I have a beautiful granddaughter named Tori who loves dandelions. She called them her happy flowers. Every time we would go into the yard, Tori would run and pick lots of dandelions. She calls them her happy love flowers. Tori would bring me a bouquet of these happy love flowers, and I would put them in my pocket. Each time, she said, "I love you, Gega!" Ten minutes later, she would be back with another handful of dandelions. I would always hug her each time. Her mom would come and get her to go home. We hugged and said, "See you later."

That night when I took off my jeans and emptied my pockets, I found a pocketful of love flowers. What we might see as a weed in our life might very well be a love flower from God. Dandelions have yellow faces, and we should be joyful in Jesus. They grow everywhere. We should be sharing Jesus everywhere we go. The roots of a dandelion are deep, and so we should be rooted deep in Jesus. When dandelions mature, you can blow on the seeds, and they go everywhere. We should be spreading the good seeds of the Gospel everywhere we go. The next time you see a dandelion, think of it as a love flower, especially if it is in the hands of a child.

Ride for a Stranger

Your ears shall hear a voice behind you
saying, "This is the way; walk in it."
—Isaiah 30:21 NKJV

Daddy was in a rest home, and my daughter and I went to see him. When we were leaving, one of the men who worked at the rest home asked if we could give him a ride to McDonald's. He got in the car, and we started talking, and I asked him about his relationship with Jesus. He said that he didn't know Jesus.

I got to McDonald's. The doors had the safety lock on them, and the man tried to get out. I smiled and said that I should keep him in the car until he found Jesus. I was kidding, but he looked scared. I unlocked the doors, and he ran to McDonald's. I am sure that he told the people about the two white women who held him hostage for Jesus. The urgency of knowing Jesus is mega important. We do not know when Jesus is going to call us home. Hopefully the stranger remembered the seeds of the Gospel that were shared.

Do you know Jesus? Are you sure of your eternity with Jesus?

My Gaga

Lo, children are a heritage of the Lord and
the fruit of the womb is his reward.
—Psalm 127:3 NKJV

Emmy is my other four-year-old granddaughter. She lives in South Carolina, and I don't get to see her as much as the one next door. We visit as much as we can, and she comes to see us. She calls me *Gaga*. One day we were sitting at a table in a restaurant, and a little girl said, "Hey, Gaga." Emmy did not like that, and she said, "She is my Gaga, not yours."

We get very jealous over the people we love. Do you know that God is jealous over you? He loves you so much. If God had a refrigerator, our picture would be taped on the front of it. He deserves our love for all that he has done for us.

Strawberries and God

*But my God shall supply your needs according
to his riches to glory by Christ Jesus.*
—Philippians 4:19 NKJV

We need to always have our heart ears attuned to God. Listening to God helps us meet people's needs and blesses us as we reach out to others. I had stopped at a fruit stand to pick up a container of strawberries. The strawberries were beautiful. There was an elderly woman sitting in the car. I spoke to her as I started back to my car with the strawberries. She said, "Those are beautiful strawberries. I wish I could get some today. I just got out of the hospital with heart surgery." I put my berries in my car, and I heard God say, *Go and buy her a container of berries and tell her they are from Me.*

I walked back to the stand and brought a basket of berries for the woman. I walked back to the car and gave them to her. I said, "These strawberries are from Jesus." She had tears in her eyes and thanked me. You see, it wasn't just the strawberries; it was the touch from Jesus. She needed that touch for encouragement. We need to always listen to Jesus. If we don't, two people lose the blessings: you and the person you were to help.

Miss Virginia and the Twins

Blessed is he that considereth the poor, the
Lord will deliver him in times of trouble.
—Psalm 41:1 NKJV

I meet many wonderful people through the ministry. One night, Miss Virginia came in. She was seventy years old. She had two-year-old twin girls with her. Her husband had just passed away. The twin girls were from one of her family members who got into trouble. Miss Virginia could not stand the thought of the girls being put in foster homes. The girls were very active, but Miss Virginia was very patient with them. Just because she was seventy years old, she knew that God was not finished with her.

She came to the ministry looking help for clothes and diapers for the girls. One of the girls looked very sad and did not smile. She said that this one had not smiled since she had come to live with Miss Virginia. I went over to the little girl, and I started singing "Jesus Loves Me" to her, and she smiled. She was little, but the name of Jesus was soothing. God doesn't call us to retire; He calls us to work until He comes to take us home. Where would these precious little girls be if Miss Virginia had said, "I am too old to take care of two little girls"? Miss Virginia is a home missionary. Are you?

The Gift

*Delight yourself in the Lord and He shall
give you the desires of your heart.*
—Psalm 37:4 NKJV

We had a beautiful daughter named Heidi. I carried Heidi for the full term. One week before she was born, the doctor told me something was wrong. He sent me to Chapel Hill and had some tests done. They told me that she had an extra chromosome, and this completely turned the inside of Heidi's body wrong. Organs were in the wrong place and not formed. He asked me if I wanted to abort her, and the answer was no. She was born on October 19. She was beautiful on the outside but so many health issues on the inside. They put her in intensive care. We stayed in the hospital for four days. The doctor came in and told me I could go home the next day, but Heidi would have to stay. They did not give her much chance of living. I prayed, "Dear God, please make Heidi well enough to go home, or please take her to heaven. I can't leave her."

God woke me up in the middle of the night and told me to go and hold Heidi. I struggled to get out of bed (I was still sore from the C-section). I held on the pump pole and walked to the intensive care unit. I held her and told her how much I loved her and that Jesus was coming to take her home. I kissed her and went back to my room. In about an hour, Jesus came as light filled my room. He said, *I have Heidi. She is well and will wait for you in heaven.* I went home, and I missed her so much.

We had a funeral, and the children sang "Jesus Loves Me." A little while later, we went to pay the funeral bill. The director of the funeral home said, "Your bill is paid in full. The person who paid it does not want you to know who did it." Even in our hard and sad times, Jesus blessed us. That act of kindness took a huge hardship off us.

Not-So-Good Chocolate

Set your mind on things above,
not on things on earth.
—Colossians 3:2 NKJV

My grandma loved me, and she spoiled me. I was named after her, and I was her first granddaughter. My grandma would save me a piece of chocolate candy each week. It was always in the top drawer of her dresser in her room. One day I went to Grandma's house and headed for the top drawer. I found a whole box of little square chocolates. I ate the entire box. A little while later, I felt sick and had to go to the outhouse a lot. Grandma asked me what was wrong. I told her I found the candy squares in her top drawer. She told me that was not the candy she had for me. I had eaten a whole box of Ex-Lax.

I often think of that experience. The medicine had the appearance of chocolate candy, but looks can be deceiving. Many times the world gives a counterfeit for what is truly good. There were consequences for my choice. There are consequences for the wrong decisions we make daily.

Speaking in Tongues

Your ears shall hear a voice behind you
saying, This is the way; walk in it.
—Isaiah 30:21 NKJV

My grandson Cole and I went to Wendy's for lunch. We ordered a Frosty, and a Spanish-speaking lady came over the microphone. We could not understand what she was saying. My grandson Cole looked at me and said, "Gega, is that lady speaking in tongues?" I smiled and explained to him that she was Spanish and that she was speaking Spanish. How many times do we try to explain what we cannot understand?

Ginna

The Lord your God himself crosses over
before you… He will be with you; He
will not leave you nor forsake you.
—Deuteronomy 31:3 NKJV

One of our first clients in the pregnancy ministry was a fifteen-year-old girl. She was pregnant and trying to make a choice. Her family was encouraging her to abort the baby. We talked, and she chose life for her baby. We helped her with her beautiful baby girl. She worked hard at being a good mom and made good grades at school. She finished high school and went on to college while taking care of her child. God sent her a godly husband, and she now has two more children. Her first child is smart and loves Jesus a lot and shares with all she meets. She chose life, and she was blessed by this precious gift from God. It was a hard road, but she made it with Jesus in her heart. Making the right choice is not always easy, but it is worth it in the large scope of things.

What Looked Like a Failure Became a Blessing

For of Him and through Him and to Him
are all things, to whom be glory forever.
—Romans 11:36 NKJV

I was asked to speak at a women's conference in a break-out section. I did not have many people to come to the section. I decided to find out where the ladies were, and I went to them. I went to lunch and gave all the ladies one of my books. I got an opportunity to witness and pray with individuals in the lunchroom. I went expecting the ladies to come to me, but God took me to the ladies. It was awesome. Don't fuss or fret when things don't work out the way you had hoped. God always has a better plan.

Blonde Wife

O taste and see that the Lord is good.
—Psalm 34:8 NKJV

I have a handsome grandson name Cole. He was six years old at the time of this conversation.

He was talking to Papa Ed one day. He said, "Papa, I want to marry a blonde-haired girl when I get big."

I said, "Cole, you need a red-haired girl. We make good wives." I said this to him because I am redheaded.

He looked at me and smiled. His answer was, "Oh no, Gega, redheads are too much trouble."

I laughed. I am praying that God gives him the godly woman he needs, whether it is a redhead or a blonde. God knows best what we need.

Sitting in Front of the Abortion Client

Pray without ceasing.
—1 Thessalonians 5:17

I was sitting in front of the abortion clinic in Fayetteville with the Life RV. We were hoping that some of the women who were going into the abortion clinic would come to us. We are a nation that has been blessed by God. God says children are a gift from God. Why in our country have we become so selfish and chose to kill our children? Our laws even condone this killing act. God's law is that we should not commit murder, but we kill thousands every day in America. As I watched these women come out of the abortion clinic, I saw pain.

One woman sat down on the ground and started crying. Another one was holding on to a tree with pain on her face. Another young woman was angry and hit the steering wheel. The abortions did not take care of their problem; it only intensified it. Many of the women were alone; the man who got them pregnant was nowhere to be found. I wept for these lost women whose choice was abortion. There is more than one victim in abortion. The baby dies, but so does a part of the mother.

Our nation will be judged for killing our sons and daughters. God punished Israel for sacrificing their children. As Christians, we can no longer sit on the sidelines and say that we do not know that abortion is murder. In Proverbs 24:11, God says we are not going to stand before Him and say we did not know it was a sin. God has told us what is true, and it is found in His Word. What are you going to do with the truth? We can in Jesus's name make a difference—one mom and one baby at a time.

Heartache

For He Himself has said, "I will never leave you nor forsake you."
—Hebrews 13:5 NKJV

I volunteer at a crisis pregnancy center. We had a young woman come in who was considering abortion. She had been raped by seven men when she was drunk one night, and now she was pregnant. She did not know who the father was. She was hopeless. I talked to her and explained that the child did not sin and didn't deserve death. The men and her drunken state were the sin. God created the child, and He is the author of life and death. I shared with her that it would help her healing if she chose life. She said, "Miss Helen, if I have this child, every time I look at the baby, I will remember the rape and the sin." I told her she needed to trust God with that part. "I promise you, when you look at your baby, you will see the image of God." She did keep the baby girl, and she named her Anna. She told me that every time she looks at Anna, she only sees a gift from God. Rape is bad. If you abort, it's like a second rape. God can and will bring good out of stinking, rotten things if we turn them over to Him.

The Head Woman

The Lord is far from the wicked but He
hears the prayer of the righteous.
—Proverbs 15:29 NKJV

There is a manager at the local abortion clinic in our community. She is called the head woman. She drives very expensive cars all bought by the blood money that she has made on the death of innocent babies. She has been doing this for thirty years. Can you imagine how many children she has killed? The other day, we were ministering outside the abortion clinic. We saw twenty young ladies go into the clinic. Later on, we watched as they came out broken and hurting. Oh, the sadness! I just wanted to take each one into my arms and tell them that Jesus loves them. We are not allowed on the abortion property, so I had to watch from the other side of the road. The manager of the abortion clinic has a hate wall with pictures of the pro-life people on it. I am sure that pictures of me and my husband are on the hate wall. I did not put her on a hate wall at the center; I have put her on the *prayer wall*. This woman needs Jesus. Jesus can come into her life and change the overseer of abortions to live in ministry. She will have a story to tell. Please pray for the people who perform abortions. Pray that Jesus will change hearts.

A Divine Appointment at the Chinese Restaurant

*Always pursue what is good both
for yourselves and for all.*
—1 Thessalonians 5:15 NKJV

Divine appointments are everywhere when you live for Jesus. My dad was in the rest home, and I left there to go and get some lunch for one of the nurses who helped Dad. I decided to go to the Chinese restaurant. I walked in and placed my order and started talking to a woman who was waiting for her food. Her name was Ann. I shared with her about the crisis pregnancy center and how we helped young women choose life for their babies. Ann shared that her hometown needed a life ministry. We talked more and set up an appointment to meet and see what we could do together. I love the way that God works. Ann did start one in her town, and it is doing well. A chance meeting? Absolutely not. It was a *divine appointment*. Look around you. God has divine appointments for you also.

The Runaway

The fear of the Lord is the beginning of wisdom.
—Psalm 111:10 NKJV

I taught kindergarten for forty years. I love teaching five-year-olds. They were so unpredictable. I had a student in my room named Scott. Scott was a handful. One day, he decided that he wanted to go home in the middle of the day, so he ran away from school. He lived five miles from the school. We searched everywhere. The principal took his car and drove down the road looking for Scott. The principal found him on the road to his house. He had walked three miles. The principal punished Scott. The parents thought it was funny, until he decided to play that trick on them. He disappeared at home; they looked for him a half day. They even called in the police. No one could find him. The police decided to drain the pond near their house. Scott walked out of the house. He had been hiding under his bed all day. The parents were glad to see him. They hugged and kissed him, and then they punished him. It was not funny this time. That was Scott's last runaway adventure. Are you a runaway from God? He loves you so much.

Reading Tub

All your children shall be taught by the Lord,
and great shall be the peace of your children.
—Isaiah 54:13 NKJV

I taught kindergarten for forty years. I had a reading tub in my classroom. It was a real tub made of cast iron and weighed about four hundred pounds. I added cushions and quilts and lots of pillows. The kids loved the reading tub. It was a reading tub and also turned into a napping place at naptime. Many times, I still see the kindergarten kids who are grown up, and they tell me that their favorite part of kindergarten was the reading tub. When I retired from teaching, I took the reading tub home with me and made a garden tub out of it. It makes a great flower bed. It is a unique way to keep memories alive. Simple things in life are sometimes the best things. If you get an opportunity, get a favorite book and sit in your tub. Make your own memories.

Summer Sister

All your children shall be taught by the Lord,
and great shall be the peace of your children.
—Isaiah 54:13 (NKJV)

My granddaughter Emmy was three years old when her parents decided to take a young girl from Russia for the summer. The girl was an orphan, and she was given an opportunity to travel to a Christian family for the summer. Emmy's parents told her to share Jesus and her toys with her guest. Emmy told them that she would share Jesus, but she hopes that her summer sister wouldn't want to play with her toys. How many times have we said we would share Jesus but not if it cost something? We need to go the extra mile to share Christ, and sometimes it costs. Remember it cost Jesus all the way to the cross.

Chicken Pox

Get wisdom! Get understanding!
—Proverbs 4:5 NKJV

I love kindergarten children, who have such an innocence to them. I was teaching kindergarten, and I noticed that Susie had big spots popping out on her face, and they were everywhere. I told her we had to call her mom because she had chicken pox. We started walking over to the office, and I told Susie that she had chicken pox. Mom was going to pick her up. Susie started crying and said, "Mrs. Rogers, I ain't been near any chickens." I often wonder why they called them chicken pox. We have to be sure to explain the facts because names can be misleading.

School Grandma

Delight yourself in the Lord and He shall
give you the desires of your heart.
—Psalm 37:4 NKJV

I taught kindergarten for forty years, and I loved it. It was my mission field. I still go to my daughter's class each week to volunteer. I love seeing their bright, shiny faces. They call me grandma. I always try to bake them a treat. I love reading to them and doing special activities with them. They all run to hug me when I come in. I have been doing this for four years. I hear students from the third, second, and first grades call me grandma when I go down the hall. I miss teaching, but this gives me a sweet taste of loving on five-year-olds. There is always a way to make a difference in this world. Ask God, and He will provide a blessing for you and others.

Volunteer Story

*For in time of trouble, He shall
hide me in His pavilion.*
—Psalm 27:5 NKJV

I have a volunteer who works with me at the center. He was a soldier. He didn't care to know Jesus. On one of his deployment, he was blown up with a roadside bomb. He lost hearing, some sight, got metal in his head, back, arms, and legs. He stayed in the hospital for eight months. They were sure that he would not live. They called his mom to say goodbye. God had a bigger plan.

During the time in the hospital, he blamed God for blowing him up. He finally was discharged from the hospital, and he moved into a house. Next door to him was a Christian couple who loved on him and showed him Jesus. They didn't preach; they lived Christ. He wanted what they had, and he came to know Christ as his Savior. His belief in Christ caused his wife to leave him. He is now working in the church and studying the Word. He volunteers at the center and is a big blessing at the crisis pregnancy center. He is a blessing and on fire for the Lord.

Many times we have to go through deep valleys so the Lord can get our attention. I asked him the other day, "Would you go through all that the pain and suffering again to find Jesus?" He said, "I would. Jesus is worth it all."

Do You Have to Go?

Let all that you do be done with love.
—1 Corinthians 16:14 NKJV

Tori was three years old, and Cole was six years old. I was on my way to the pregnancy center to help the moms and babies. I told the kids I had to leave and that I would see them later. I walked to the door, and both Tori and Cole said, "Do you have to leave, Gega?" I told them yes because I needed to help babies that needed clothes and diapers. Both Tori and Cole blocked the door. Tori said, "Okay, let me help." She ran over and picked up a diaper that was left over when she was a baby. She gave it to me and said, "This is for God's babies."

How many adults feel the same way about these children who don't always come into the world with mom and dad married? Are these children still precious in God's sight? The answer is *yes*! The parents had the sex, but God created the child, and this child has a purpose and is part of a divine plan.

A Letter from a Friend

A Friend loves at all times.
—Proverbs 17:17

Helen,

This morning, as I was praying, the Holy Spirit spoke this into my heart, so I wanted to share this with you. You are such an inspiration to me and my faith. I thank God for putting us together.

Love,
Deanna

Regarding Helen

She is My faithful servant. She thinks about Me before herself. She is quick to obey, and in her heart is much love. Great is her reward. She is diligent to follow Me. I smile at her ways. She has fun and takes pleasure in the assignments I give her. She is a breath of fresh air to My nostrils. She is pure and genuine. She has great favor with Me. I long to talk with her because she is always about My business. Don't let appearance fool you. She is clothed with greatness, majesty, and roy-alty. She has fought hard for My concerns. Tell her not to worry about her legacy; it will not die. I did not put her in the position she is in to have the enemy steal, kill, or destroy it. Her legacy will continue. I will raise up a generation that will love and will save the babies. Tell her to rest and to not grow weary, for in due season, she will reap the harvest!

Diapers for Colombia, South America

Everyone helped his neighbor, and said
to his brother, "Be of good courage!"
—Isaiah 4:6 NKJV

I have a friend named Anna. She came into the pregnancy center and asked if we could help start a crisis pregnancy center in her small village outside of Colombia. She had married a soldier, and they were stationed in Fayetteville. She was upset because Planned Parenthood had moved into her village, and they were killing the babies through abortion. She asked if I could help her start a crisis pregnancy center in the village. I told her we could. We named the center Jesus Loves the Little Children. Her sister is passing out diapers and baby clothes to the young mothers in need. They are also learning of Jesus's love for them and their babies. The Agape Pregnancy Support Services sends diapers and baby clothes to Anna, and she mails them to South America.

One day she called to tell me she needed diapers for the babies. I prayed that God would bless us, and He did—with 145 packs of diapers. We were able to get the diapers to Anna, and she was able to bless the moms in South America. God tells us to get out of our comfort zone and go to our neighbor even if they are in another country. I have some beautiful pictures of young Spanish moms holding the baby items we sent. We would have missed a blessing if we had not listened.

Hope

Through love serve one another.
—Galatians 5:13 NKJV

I am the director of several crisis pregnancy centers. I see lots of clients from all walks of life. One day, Miss Hattie came into the center. She had just picked up a three-month-old little girl named Hope. She needed items for the baby. This little girl was so sad. Hattie said she had never seen her smile. Hope had been through so much to be so young. I got the stuff together for Hope and handed it to Miss Hattie. I went over to Hope, and I prayed for her. Then I started singing "Jesus Loves Me" to her. She looked at me and gave me the biggest smile you have ever seen. I smiled and said, "Jesus always bring joy to our heart and face." I told Miss Hattie to sing praises to Jesus over her and pray for her scars.

Do You Have a Toothbrush, Mister?

Let all that you do be done with love.
—1 Corinthians 16:14 NKJV

We met a missionary couple through a missions conference. She was telling me about the time that a family came to her house to get food for their family. The missionary gave the bag of food to the family and set it in the back of their truck. The little four-year-old girl climbed up in the back of the truck and started looking through the bag. She looked at the missionary and said, "Mister, do you have a toothbrush in here? I need one." The missionary went out to the local store and got her a toothbrush.

The Jenkins, Kentucky, area is in great need of dental health. Since then, they have started a dental clinic once a month with visiting dentists. We collected over 1,200 toothbrushes and toothpastes to help meet the need. Jesus tells us that if we know a need and we do nothing, we sin. Look around you! What are the needs of the ones you meet?

Teach the Word

For God so loved the world that he
gave his only begotten son.
—John 3:16 NKJV

My grandson was at church in his Sunday school class. He had just learned John 3:16. The pastor asked him to share the scripture during service. After church, a little five-year-old girl told Cole she wanted to learn that verse. Mom went looking for Cole and found him in the middle of the floor teaching the little girl John 3:16. My daughter had tears in her eyes as she listened to Cole teaching the verse. We should always be ready to share the Word with all we meet, no matter how old or young we are. To whom have you shared the Word today?

Sam Houston

Through love, serve one another.
—Galatians 5:13 NKJV

The youth group of our church went to West Virginia on a mission trip. We did backyard Bible clubs and ministered in a Woman's Prison. These women were pregnant and were allowed to have their babies and keep them for 16 months. After that they had to call a family member to come and get their child. There was such sadness. We took diapers and clothes for the babies and had a Bible study with them. In the evening, we went to the local park to have a Bible club and serve refreshments. We had a little boy to come to VBS. He was six years old, and his name was Sam Houston. Sam Houston was tough. He chased the other children with a tree branch. He used swear words.

When it was time to go, my husband noticed that Sam was walking home alone. He asked if he could walk with him. Sam said, "But, mister, I do this all the time." When Ed got him home, Sam's dad was sitting on the porch drunk. He didn't say a word to Sam. Sam told Ed that his mother had left him. No wonder Sam had such a hard time dealing with life. Many times, when we see children or teenagers who are angry, there is a broken home somewhere. I think of Sam often and pray that there will be Christian people in his life to show him the way. Do you have any Sams around you?

Kids with Hearts

Let all that you do be done with love.
—1 Corinthians 16:14 NKJV

Miss Bessie is my missionary friend in Jenkins, Kentucky. She lives in a very poor area in the Appalachian Mountains. Bessie and her husband minister to the people in that area. Most of the men in that area have lost their coal-mining jobs, and with, that their livelihood for their family. Bessie has two grandchildren who live nearby. One day she received a call from the local school. Her grandson had just won a new bike in some kind of contest at the school. He gave his new bike away to a child who did not have a bike. He said his old bike would do for him. The teacher just wanted to make sure that this was all right for him to give the new bike away. The mom and grandmom were elated that their son and grandson had been so generous. This child had been raised in giving to others.

Miss Bessie's granddaughter was just as generous. Her granddad had given her a new doll with clothes for Christmas. A woman came to the door of the mission house and told Bessie that her (the woman's) granddaughter had come to stay with her, and she didn't have anything to give her for Christmas. Miss Bessie told her she didn't have anything either. Miss Bessie's granddaughter heard her from the other room. She boxed up her new baby doll with the clothes and took it to the woman. What a true Christmas heart that both of these children have. Children copy what they see. If they see us sharing and reaching out to others, they will do the same. What are your children seeing?

The Couple

Through love, serve one another.
—Galatians 5:13 NKJV

A couple walked into the pregnancy center unwed, pregnant, and lost. He was adopted when he was little, her family was dysfunctional and very lost. Both families told them to abort this baby. We helped them with parenting classes, baby items, car seat, and lots of love and witnessing. They both went back to school. They gave their son life. They continued to stop by after their son was born so I could see how much he was growing. They moved away, and I lost contact with them for about two years. One night I got a call at the center from Sue. They had gotten married, gotten saved, finished school, and now had two sons. Sue is a social worker helping other young struggling mothers. Greg is a manager of a local restaurant. She had called just to say thank you. She said that the pregnancy center and the volunteers made a difference in her family. We should never give up on the people we meet. We may feel like they are not listening, but they are. It just takes some people longer to get to the Lord.

Worship Time with Tori

He who does not love does not
know God for God is love.
—1 John 4:8 NKJV

Tori is next to my youngest granddaughter, and she loves Jesus. Everywhere we go, she will break out in song praising God. We were walking on the beach; it was a beautiful day. My four-year-old granddaughter was beside me when, all of a sudden, she started singing praises to God. We both held hands and praised God together. It was an awesome time of worship. Another day, we had gone shopping at Walmart, just Tori and me. She looked at me and said, "Gega, these people need Jesus." She started singing "Jesus Loves Me" and the "BBle" (she left out the *i*) just as loudly as she could. I helped her. People turned toward us and smiled. She was sharing Christ. There is no excuse that we are not sharing Christ as we go. There are opportunities everywhere.

Soles for Souls

Through love, serve one another.
—Galatians 5:13 NKJV

I have a missionary friend who lives in the Kentucky in the Appalachians Mountains. The town is in a poverty-stricken area. All the coal miners lost their jobs due to the closing of the coal mines. Families were in need. Miss Bessie and Mr. Lester share God's love through many missions in that area. Miss Bessie called me and asked me if we could get some new tennis shoes for the children in Jenkins, Kentucky. Many of the kids are wearing shoes that are too small, and some are wearing their older sibling's shoes that are too big. I put out a mission call for my area and asked for new tennis shoes from tots to teenager sizes. We loaded up Mr. Gene's trailer with 1,500 pairs of new tennis shoes, and we headed for Jenkins. It was awesome. We passed out the shoes at the park. The families were lined up all the way down the street two hours early.

The first young man came up to me and asked me for a pair of tennis shoes. I asked him his name. His name was Hayden. I asked him what size shoes he wore. He said he did not know, that he was wearing his grandma's shoes. We found him a pair of shoes, and he was so happy. I told him they were Jesus's shoes, and he looked at me with a questioning look. I said, "These are Jesus's shoes, and Jesus wants to take you to good places with them." I explained to him that when you have Jesus in your heart, He will guide your steps. He said he had heard about this Jesus but didn't know how to get Him. I told Hayden that I knew Jesus personally, and I could introduce him to Jesus. We talked, and Hayden asked Jesus into his heart. I was crying, grandma was crying, and Hayden was crying. We gave him a new Bible. He held the Bible like it was gold. He started to leave but turned around and took out of his pocket a tattered wallet. Inside, he had two pennies. He gave the pennies to me and said, "Is this enough for Jesus?" I said, "It is enough." I still have those two pennies glued in my Bible. I would like to think that Hayden will one day be the Billy Graham for Jenkins, Kentucky. He will lead many to know Jesus Christ.

Ten Abortions

For the wages of sin is death.
—Romans 6:23 NKJV

I know a young woman who made lots of bad choices most of her life. She had twelve children and aborted ten of them. The two living children were raised by others in the family. The pain and the sin of killing ten children caught up with her. She committed suicide. Abortion kills the baby but also destroys the mom. I have met many women who have had an abortion, but I have not met one who was glad she did it. The sorrow and pain are what I hear when I counsel with these women. I call women who have aborted the *walking wounded*. We have them everywhere: they are sitting in our churches with their dark secrets.

Women who have aborted need counseling, and they need to share their story. The devil wants to keep you bound in your sin. Bringing that sin to the light will help with the healing and put the devil on the run. If you have aborted a child, it is not an unpardonable sin; it is forgivable. God loves you, and you will see that child again if you have accepted Jesus Christ as your Savior. Part of the healing from abortion is to ask God the sex of the child, name your child, and write your child a letter. Forgive yourself just as God has forgiven you.

Tori and Joy

Blessed are the people who know the joyful sound.
—Psalm 89:15 NKJV

I have a four-year-old granddaughter named Tori. She loves Jesus. She praises Him all day. I was taking a walk with her, and she started singing the Christian song "Ain't Nobody Going to Steal My Joy." Many times we allow people, circumstances, and feelings to rob us of our Jesus joy. God tells us in the Word to *rejoice*. That means to have joy over and over again. Joy means to love Jesus first, others second, and yourself last. That is the true joy.

Oh No, Not the Dentist

Be steadfast, immovable, always
abounding in the work of the Lord.
—1 Corinthians 15:58 NKJV

Going to the dentist is not my favorite thing to do. Dr. Sloan calls me his favorite coward. I broke a tooth and went to the dentist. It had to be fixed by root canal and a crown. I sat in the chair a long time. It got me thinking that in heaven there are no root canals, and the crowns we get are the ones we have earned on earth. These are crowns of the good things we have done for Jesus. The most wonderful thing about getting these crowns is we get to throw them at Jesus's feet in His honor. Wow!

Fatherless

Eye has not seen, nor ear heard…the things which
God has prepared for those who love Him.
1 Corinthians 2:9 NKJV

Hunter was another young man who came through the lines in Kentucky when we were passing out new tennis shoes to the children in a poverty area. He was with his grandmother. He was so sad and looked down at his feet. Grandma shared that Hunter's dad had died recently and that his mom had left Hunter. We gave him some new shoes and shared about heaven and Jesus with him. I told him that there is a Heavenly Father who would never leave him or forsake him. I told him about Jesus, who had given His life for us all so that we can one day be with Him in heaven. He accepted Jesus, and he had the biggest smile on his face. His grandma was crying, and so was I. We gave him a Bible, and he walked away a different person than the one minutes before. Jesus is our only hope in this world. There is too much sorrow and sadness, and we cannot make it without Jesus. We will not make it without Jesus.

Praying All My Life

Delight yourself in the Lord, and He shall
give you the desires of your heart.
—Psalm 37:4 NKJV

One of the children who came through the shoe line in Jenkins, Kentucky, was a little girl named Isabelle. She was four years old and asked if we had any light-up Frozen shoes her size. I looked and looked through all the shoes. As I looked, I prayed that there would be a size 5 pair of light-up Frozen shoes for Isabelle. I found one pair, and I could not see the size of the shoe. I put them on her feet, and she started dancing. They were just the right size. Thank You, Jesus. Isabelle looked at me and said, "I have prayed all my life for light-up Frozen shoes, and Jesus answered my prayer." We had over one thousand pairs of shoes on that table, and only God could make sure that Isabelle's faith would grow even as a four-year-old. What are you praying for? God has the answer for you, and it is just the right size.

Real Bible

Your ears shall hear a voice behind you
saying, "This is the way; walk in it."
—Isaiah 30:21 NKJV

The Kentucky mission trip showed us so much the mighty hand of God. We were passing out shoes and also Bibles to the children in the poverty area. One young man asked if he could have a real Bible. He had never had one before. He was so excited when we gave him his Bible. He walked away reading the Bible. He was excited to be in the Word. Are you excited when you read the Word? It is a love letter from God and a road map for life.

Exceedingly More

Delight yourself in the Lord, And He shall
give you the desires of your heart.
—Psalm 37:4 NKJV

Our goal when we went on our mission trip to Jenkins, Kentucky, was to take 1,500 pairs of new tennis shoes sizes from tots to teenagers. The area in the Appalachian Mountains is very poor. Most of the children in this area had never had new tennis shoes. Many of them were wearing hand-me-down shoes from family members. Miss Bessie, the missionary in that area, contacted us and asked if we would bring new tennis shoes. We were to leave the next day for Kentucky, and I had 997 pairs of tennis shoes. I prayed, "Dear Lord, I need to have tennis shoes for 1,500 children, and I only have 997. Would You please bless us with the rest before we leave in the morning?" The next day, as we were loading the truck for Kentucky, several groups showed up with new tennis shoes. I counted and added them to the rest—we had 1,500 pairs of brand-new tennis shoes. I have found in my walk with Jesus that He always does exceedingly more than we can ask or imagine. He is an on-time God!

Grace

The Lord will command His loving kindness
in the daytime, And in the night His song shall
be with me—A prayer to the God of my life.
                                —Psalm 42:8 NKJV

My precious grandchildren were in the car with me. We were just coming back from an appointment. We stopped by McDonald's to get lunch. I turned around and said to my four-year-old granddaughters, "Y'all say grace." They looked at me, and both said the word *grace* at the same time. They were used to saying a prayer before the meal, and they were not sure of the word *grace*. I explained it to them, and they said grace for the McDonald's food. We have to be careful when we use church words sharing Christ. An unchurched person may not understand some of our Christian words. Always use simple words and simply tell your testimony.

Two for One Sale

For with God nothing is impossible.
—Luke 1:37 NKJV

I have been sharing about some of our mission trips to Kentucky. We started taking toys for one thousand children at Christmas. Everyone was collecting toys. I saw an ad for toys at the local CVS for two-for-one sale. I was so excited. I went in to the store and got $600 worth of toys for $300. The next day, someone gave me some extra money for more toys. I went back to the CVS. The sale was off. I was sad. I decided that you have not if you do not ask. I found the manager and shared with him why I needed the toys. He looked at me and said, "The sale is still on for you. Get what you need." I was so happy! I got $900 worth of toys for $450. God is the same way. We need to ask God for what we need. Our Abba Daddy wants to bless us because He loves us so much.

Oranges and Oranges

The Lord is my shepherd. I shall not want.
—Psalm 23:1 NKJV

The mission trip to Kentucky was coming together. We were taking toys to the children in the Appalachian Mountains. I wanted to take some fresh fruit to the children. I needed seven hundred oranges, and that is what I prayed for and thanked God for. Someone gave me apples, and I continued to make the goodie bags, knowing that God would provide the oranges. On the day before we were to leave, a man on a truck drove up and had boxes in the back. He said, "God told me to bring you seven hundred oranges, and I have them here." It was just the amount needed. This man had listened to God, and now we were being blessed, and we could now bless the children in the poor area of Kentucky. God is always faithful. He loved the children of Kentucky, the man who gave us the oranges, and me. Always walk in faith. We have an Abba Daddy who will meet our needs if we are faithful.

Sarah and the Candy

Let my prayer be set before you as incense.
—Psalm 141:3 NKJV

Our mission trip to Jenkins, Kentucky, was to bless the children of the Appalachian Mountains with a "Happy Birthday, Jesus" party. We had around one thousand children to come through to receive gifts. An eight-year-old girl came through named Sarah. She had a small gift wrapped in her hand. I unwrapped it, and it was a bowl of peppermint candy. She thanked me for coming to share with the children of her town. Her grandma told us that she had severe heart problems and was scheduled for heart surgery the following week. I prayed for Sarah. We learned later on that Sarah is doing well. Her physical heart was broken, but her spiritual heart was good. All is well in Jesus.

Jesus and the Drum Set

I will bless the Lord of all times; His praise
shall continually be in my mouth.
—Psalm 34:1 NKJV

Many times during the year, different groups will give baby showers for the pregnancy ministry. A kindergarten teacher contacted me and asked if I could come to a baby shower the kindergarten kids had planned. I walked into the class, and the children were so excited. They started presenting me with the gifts that they had picked out for baby Jesus. One child gave me diapers and wipes. Another child gave a diaper bag; and others gave toiletries, baby clothes, blankets, and bottles.

There was one boy who still had his gift. I motioned for him to come to me. He walked up and handed me his gift for Jesus. I said, "Let's open this gift together." Inside the present, there was a drum set. He said, "I got him a drum set. I know Jesus loves music." I assured him that Jesus does love music, and He would love the drum set. He smiled and walked away, happy over his gift. I am sure that Jesus was happy with the gift also because it came from the heart. It made me think of the Little Drummer Boy and how he gave his best for Jesus. Have you given Jesus the special gift of your heart?

Blessing from a Stranger

*I will praise You, O Lord, with my whole
heart; I will tell of all Your marvelous works.*
—Psalm 9:1 NKJV

Finances get tight sometimes. I am a volunteer director of three pregnancy centers in three counties. I am a retired kindergarten teacher,
and my husband was pastoring at a small church. Money was tight.
I sent my son to the local pharmacy to pick up his medicine. I told
him I would try to get mine later. The pharmacist asked Tom if he
wanted to pick up his mom's meds. Tom told him he didn't have
enough money to purchase my meds. There was a stranger in line
behind my son. She said, "I want to bless your mom. I will pay for
the medicine." She paid for my medicine, and I to this day do not
know who she was. She was a blessing. Have you blessed someone
today?

Who Prays for You?

Then Jesus spoke to them saying, "I am the
light of the world. He who follows me shall not
walk in darkness, but have the light of life."
—John 8:12 NKJV

I meet a lot of young women who come into the center. Many of them are so lost, pregnant, and lonely. One night, Christina came into the center. She was pregnant, boyfriend gone, mother dead, dad sick and out of work. She had so much burden. I started talking to her, and I asked, "Who prays for you, Christina?" She turned toward me with tears in her eyes and said, "Nobody prays for me, Miss Helen. I don't have any Christians in my family." I told her that I would pray for her right now, and I would pray for her every day. We helped her find a place to stay where she would be safe. The family took care of Christina and her baby. She now is a Christian, and she prays for her baby. We need to pray for the ones we meet right there on the spot. Some people do not have someone praying for them.

To My Friend Julie

*Seek first the kingdom of God and
His righteousness and all these
things shall be added to you.*
                        —Matthew 6:33 NKJV

To my friend Julie,

Julie, thank you being the kindest and most compassionate friend. Your love was given to all who came near you. Your family was your heart. You loved your husband and made him proud to be your husband. Your sons made your eyes shine as you looked at the young men they had become. And, oh, those precious grandchildren—you shared stories and the wonderful things they did. You always had time for them.

Julie, you loved Jesus; and many times when I would come to the store, we would praise the Lord together. Sometimes we would pray for whatever need we had in our families. You would always tell me to pray for your family. You were so proud of your family. You would ask me about the center and if there was a need. I would share some of the stories, and before I left, you had given a donation to help those in need. You made everyone who came in the store feel so welcome, and you ask about their families.

The Bible talks about a Proverbs 31 woman, and you were that woman.

You will be missed by all who knew you, Julie. We know where you are, and I believe it is your desire to see your whole family with you in heaven one day. That would be the best homecoming.

Julie, I promise to pray for your family every day. I will not tell you bye, but I will say *see you later*.

Love,
Helen Rogers

Have Courage

May He send you help from the sanctuary,
and strengthen you out of Zion.
                                        —Psalm 20:2

I believe that God wants us to stand for right and truth no matter how inconvenient it might be. There was a new curriculum being reviewed to be used in our county. It was called *Real Sex*, which was written and pushed by Planned Parenthood. It was very descriptive and almost vulgar and was to be taught in the local middle schools. I was asked to speak at the local board meeting by parents who did not want this curriculum. I only had three minutes to speak. I got to the meeting one hour early so I would be the first one to speak.

I asked the board that was responsible for all these young children if they had read the entire curriculum. My next question was, "Would you want your children and grandchildren to sit in a class listening to this garbage?" I told them that flashcards were not to be used to show sex acts but to teach reading words and math facts. I shared that children needed truth from us. I also reminded them that the abortion people who had written this curriculum had an agenda, and that was to get rich off the abortions these young people would have. I told them that young people are smart: give them truth, and they will make good choices. With this curriculum, there would be more abortions, more STDs, more babies born out of wedlock, and more depression and suicide.

I finished, and many people stood and clapped, but I noticed that the pro-choice people did not appreciate the speech. Later on, the curriculum was rejected. Praise God! Be bold. Stand for the truth—you will never regret it.

Newsletters Blessings

*My God shall supple all your need according
to His riches in glory by Christ Jesus.*
—Philippians 4:19 NKJV

Each month in the pregnancy ministry, we send out 4,400 newsletters. One day I went to pick up the newsletters with a check in hand. The man rolled out the newsletters, and I asked how much so I could write the check. The couple who owned the business said the newsletters were free. That was an $800 blessing. God is so *good*! He takes care of this life ministry through Christian people. What can you do to make a difference?

Death to Life

Your ears shall hear a voice behind you
saying, "This is the way, walk in it."
—Isaiah 30:21 NKJV

I had an eighteen-year-old girl call me and ask how much an abortion was. She already had an eleven-month-old girl and was pregnant again. Her boyfriend was in jail. She didn't have any resources. I counseled her about life by parenting her child or putting the baby up for adoption. "To abort your baby is not the right choice. It will cause you more sorrow than you can bear." We talked, and she gave me permission to call back later the next day. I called her every day for two weeks and prayed for her. We gave her a free ultrasound. She decided to parent the baby. She soon delivered a beautiful baby girl named London. She weighed six pounds and two ounces, and she was perfect. I have to tell you that there is something extraspecial about holding a baby who was almost aborted. God smiles at these little ones, and so do we. They are doing fine, and she is a good mother.

Heaven Is Very Real

The Lord is my shepherd; I shall not want
—Psalm 23:1

I have a beautiful four-year-old granddaughter named Tori. She and her four-year-old cousin Emmy love Jesus. Tori told me that she went to heaven. I asked, "What did you see there?" She said, "I saw Jesus, and He was a bright light. I also saw His Daddy, God. I also saw my brother who went to heaven when he was born. He looked a lot like my brother Cole who is with me on earth. Gega, there were lots of flowers, and Jesus said I could pick all the flowers I wanted. I danced in the flowers. I didn't want to leave heaven. Gega, when we go there, we can pick beautiful flowers and walk with Jesus."

Tori talks of heaven a lot, and I believe God gave her a glimpse of heaven. I believe God was preparing Tori for the day when her Papa Ed would die and go to heaven. He died in February, and she was a little upset that he went without her. Heaven is for real, and we need to make plans to go there.

God's Dental Plan

For with God nothing is impossible.
—Luke 1:37 NKJV

Our family befriended a young man who was having a difficult time. His mother had walked out on him and his sister when he was thirteen years old. She told him she was going to have fun. I will call the young man Steve. Steve had to have four wisdom teeth pulled, and his mother had promised to carry him to the appointment. At the last minute, she called and said she couldn't come; something had come up. My daughter said she would take him, and she did. She even took care of him after the surgery. Steve had paid $1,000 down and had agreed to pay the balance of $1,800 with monthly payments. He was working at a fast-food place, and he didn't have much money. I prayed that God would help him with the bill. He went back for a checkup, and the doctor gave him a bill that said "paid in full." God had blessed him. My daughter reminded Steve that the gift was from God. Thank You, Jesus, for the answered prayer.

Who Are We?

For you will light my lamp; The Lord my God
will enlighten my darkness… By my God I can
leap over a wall. As for God, His way is perfect.
—Psalm 18:28–30 NKJV

I am the director of several crisis pregnancy centers, and one of them is the Agape Pregnancy Support Services in Fayetteville, North Carolina. The building we are in was at one time an abortion clinic where they murdered one hundred thousand children or more. God had us purchase the building and turn it in to a crisis pregnancy center. God has really blessed the work for life in this building. One day I went to the local lumberyard to pick up something for the center. I started back to the car, and a man walked up to me and said, "Are you the Agape Center Lady?" I told him yes, I was the director. He took out his wallet and handed me a one-hundred-dollar bill.

He said to use it for the babies. When we do God's work, God will bless us in many ways.

Gaga Day

Oh, satisfy us early with your mercy, that
we may rejoice and be glad all our days!
—Psalm 90:14 NKJV

My four-year-old granddaughter Emmy is so full of life. I laugh at her sayings and the way she looks at the world. My grandchildren call me Gega or Gaga. She lives in South Carolina, and I don't get to see her as much as the other grandchildren. My husband and I made a playdate to pick Emmy up and take her to the children's museum. She was so excited. Emmy was looking forward to Friday. She told her dad, "Do you know what day tomorrow is?" Her dad said, "Yes, it is Friday." Emmy said, "No, Daddy, it is Gaga Day."

I am so blessed to have the grandchildren that I have. They love one another, and they all love Jesus. We did have a great "Gaga Day" and made lots of wonderful memories. Give your grandchild a memory day.

Blessings in a Diaper Bag

For we walk by faith, not by sight.
—2 Corinthians 5:7 NKJV

We take mission trips to Jenkins, Kentucky, to the poorest area in the Appalachian Mountains. One of our favorite trips each year is to pack diaper bags for the moms and babies. Many of these moms have nothing for their babies. We had a baby shower in the park, and we had two hundred moms come by to get diaper bags filled with baby items. We prayed over every mom who came by to get a diaper bag. One family received the girl bag, and the five-year-old brother was so excited. They took the items home and laid them on the bed to look at the baby-girl stuff. The brother touched each item and talked about how much his baby sister would like it. He looked at his mom and said, "Jesus must really love my baby sister. Look at all the pretty things He gave her." It is important that when we share and give things, we do it in Jesus's name and glory.

The Traveling Crisis Pregnancy Center

*If we walk in the light as He is in the light, we
have fellowship with one another, and the blood
of Jesus Christ His Son cleanses us form all sin.*
—1 John 1:6 NKJV

We could not be in all the places we needed to be, counseling with women with crisis pregnancies, so the Lord blessed us with an RV life van. We filled it with baby clothes, diapers, and lots of baby items. We put a big sign on the outside of the RV, and we started traveling to other counties. We set up in parking lots or churches, and we wait for the Lord to send the clients. And He does. The Gospel is shared with all who enter the RV, and baby items are also shared. God teaches us to be creative. He is creative, and if we listen to Him, we will be able to minister to more people.

We parked at a Burger King to get something to eat, and we had a couple come to the RV. We were able to help them right there in the parking lot. It is exciting to serve God.

Food-Bank Revival

My help comes from the Lord; Who made heaven
and earth. He will not allow your foot to be
moved; He who keeps you will not slumber.
—Psalm 121:2–3 NKJV

I have a friend who runs a food bank at her church. She has a Christian Jewish rabbi who comes to help her at the food bank. The other day, they were closing up, and a gentle breeze started blowing. The rabbi said, "This is the Holy Spirit moving." He shared the plan of salvation, and one person walked up and asked to be saved. In a few minutes, more came to front and asked to be saved. Thirteen people got saved that day all because the rabbi was obedient to the calling of the Holy Spirit. The Holy Spirit is always moving. We need to be open to the calling. Wow, we serve an awesome God.

Joshua Caleb

*A friend loves at all times, and a
brother is born for adversity.*
—Proverbs 17:17 NKJV

The pregnancy ministry helps meet the needs of all kinds of clients. I had a young eighteen-year-old girl who was from a different religion call to ask about making a choice for her baby. She was ten weeks pregnant and undecided about what to do with her baby. The father of the baby was a soldier, and he was deployed. She was afraid of her parents, who would have her returned to her country because she had brought shame on her family. I talked to her and asked if would like a free ultrasound. We made an appointment for her to return for the ultrasound. Sarah (not her real name) returned, and you could see a beautiful baby boy bouncing around in the womb. In one of the ultrasounds pictures, the baby had placed his hands to his chin in prayer mode. I told her he was praying to Jesus. She took the ultrasound picture and went to make copies to send to the father of her baby. She chose life for her son that day.

Joe and Sarah made plans to marry. She knew she had to get away from her family. Plans were made to get her to a safe place. The day before Mother's Day, someone told Sarah's mom that she was pregnant. Sarah's mother made her daughter get in the car against her will and took her to an abortion clinic. That precious little boy died that day. I cried for three days over the death of this child. I asked God to show us what we needed to do to give value to this precious child. I named him Joshua Caleb

God led us to start a traveling crisis pregnancy center We were in a building for a while right across from the abortion clinic while he died. We are fighting the battle for life right in the face of the enemy. I feel like David, and abortion is the Goliath. We pray for the closing of the abortion clinic, and I would love to own the building for a dollar one day so we can start a crisis pregnancy center where so many babies have died. The battle is intense, and we will continue to fight for all the other Joshua Calebs to live the life that God has planned for them.

Sunflower Child

For with God nothing is impossible.
—Luke 1:37 NKJV

Tori is my precious four-year-old granddaughter, and she loves to help me in my flower garden. She gets so excited when we get ready to plant seeds. We were planting a sunflower bed. We took the seeds, and she started to plant them. I told her that we needed to pray over the seeds so that God would grow them high. She prayed over her handful of seeds. She sat down in front of the sunflower bed and said, "Gega, sit down here with me, and let's watch the sunflower grow." I explained to her that it takes time for the seeds to grow. Our job is to water the seeds and keep the weeds out. She was faithful to come every day and measure the plants to see how much they had grown. The plants grew big and beautiful. Tori enjoyed picking the sunflowers and giving them to people. We also plant seeds as we go. We plant the seeds of Jesus Christ, and if we are faithful, there will be a beautiful harvest one day.

Where Are the Five Hundred?

Rejoice always pray without ceasing, in
everything give thanks; for this is the
will of God in Christ Jesus for you.
—1 Thessalonians 5:16–18 NKJV

I am learning to be obedient as the Lord asked. I have found that if I am obedient the first time he asked, I would see the blessings faster. One day, God told me to plan a women's conference for five hundred people with speakers, music, food, and lots of prayer. I rented the local community school center. I got the food and the speakers for the day. I prayed over the upcoming event and knew that God was going to do mighty things. The day we had the event, the weather turned rough with threats of tornadoes. Six o'clock came, and instead of five hundred, I had thirty people. Just before the event started, I stood at the door and prayed.

There was a teenager who had helped prepare for the conference. She came up to me and said, "Miss Helen, are you mad with God? This was a lot of work for thirty people." I told her that I had listened to God and that I had no regrets. I cannot control the weather; I can only control my obedience. The Bible says that obedience is better than sacrifice. We had an awesome time in the Lord that day, worshipping and praising Him. Everyone left better than they came.

Betrayal

Whatever you do, do it heartily, as to the
Lord and not to men, knowing that from
the Lord you will receive the reward of the
inheritance; for you serve the Lord Christ.
But he who does wrong will he be repaid for
what he has done, and there is no partiality.
—Colossians 3:23–25 NKJV

My husband, Ed, has been a pastor for most of his adult life. He loves the Lord and preaches the Lord without shame. We were called to a church that was dying. Ed accepted the call. He loved the people, visited the sick, prayed for them, and preached the whole Word. One Wednesday night, the chairman of the deacons said, "You have stabilized our church, and it is growing again. We feel you are not the shepherd for us anymore. You have done nothing wrong." My wonderful husband was crushed. He resigned from the church. Please know that it was not the entire church that wanted him to leave; it was three people with too much power. The rest of the church body cried when we left.

How do you start over again at seventy? I was angry at first; this was not God's will or way. We were walking forward knowing that God takes care of His children. Ed was betrayed by the chairman of the deacons. He thought he was a friend. Jesus was betrayed by Judas, one of His followers. After this happened to Ed, he got leukemia and died seven months later. I believe the leukemia did kill him, but I also believe he died of a broken heart. God says there will be trials and tribulations in this world, but He will never leave us nor forsake us.

Teardrop Monument

If one member suffers, all the members
suffer with it, or if one member is honored,
all the members rejoice with it.
—1 Corinthians 12:26 NKJV

My husband and I started a crisis pregnancy center in Fayetteville. The building that God called us to purchase was the old abortion clinic where more than one hundred thousand babies had died. God said He wanted to redeem it from death to life. We anointed and prayed over the building and marched around it, casting out the demons that had the building for so long. We have been here sixteen years, and God has blessed us. You see, we are not on the sunny side of town. We are in an area infested with drugs and prostitution. We are right where God wants us to be.

One of the prostitutes came to the door once and asked to sit in the children's playroom. I asked her why she wanted to do that, and her reply was, "I killed three of my children in this place with abortions." There is so much pain that goes with abortion. We have a prayer garden out front. God directed us to place a monument as a memorial to all the children who died in this place. I went to pick it out, and I chose a teardrop monument. It seemed so fitting. The monument has a picture of Jesus holding a baby in his arms. At the top of the monument, it has "In Memory of All the Children Who Were Aborted in This Place." There is also a letter on the monument that says, "Dear Mommy, I love you and I miss you. I forgive you. Will you please ask Jesus into your heart so we can be in heaven together? Love, Your Child." We have many women who will sit in the prayer garden and find peace. Please know that if you have had an abortion, God forgives, and you will see your child again.

Cheesy Bible Study

Everyone helped his neighbor, and said
to his brother, "Be of good courage!"
—Isaiah 41:6

I wrote a book called *God Loves You Better Than Mac and Cheese*. It is really a God book. This book is a one of God's daily miracles. When I got it published, I prayed that God would use it for His glory and honor. I wanted to see God take it to other states and countries. I volunteer in four counties in North Carolina. If this book was to travel, God had to do it.

We had a young couple come into the center. They had moved to Kentucky. They had previously lived in Fayetteville and did a lot of street ministry. They stopped by to see if they could get some copies of the book *God Loves You Better Than Mac and Cheese*. She explained they had moved to Kentucky where her mom was a director of a crisis pregnancy center. They shared that the book was being used with the clients and volunteers at the center in Kentucky. Another family came through and got a box of the books and took them across the United States and Mexico as they ministered to the prisoners. Only God can answer a prayer like that. It makes my heart sing.

The Power of Prayer

Rejoice always, pray without ceasing,
in everything give thanks; for this is the
will of God in Christ Jesus for you.
—1 Thessalonians 5:16–18 NKJV

I have a pastor friend, and he is very pro-life. He believes in prayer and that prayer can save lives. He and his church went to an abortion clinic one cold snowy winter day. They stood outside in the freezing cold, and they saw twelve young women walk in for abortions. They kept praying. They even got on their knees in the snow and prayed. None of the girls came out, so the pastor and his church felt that they had lost the battle for life.

One year later, they came back to pray again at the abortion clinic; and as they were praying, twelve moms with strollers with babies came up to them. They asked, "Are you the people that were praying last year outside this clinic?" The girls told the story that the year before, the Holy Spirit felt so strong on the women in the clinic when the people were praying. She said, "We all fell on our knees and said, 'We are not going to kill our babies.'" The abortion director told them they could not leave the abortion clinic until all the Christians were gone. She said, "I do not want the Christians to think that they won." God won that day, and twelve precious babies were saved because Christians prayed. Sometimes we do not know the power of our prayers until later. God hears and answers prayers.

No Sleepovers Yet

The Lord your God in your midst, the mighty
one will save; He will quiet you with His
love: He will rejoice over you with singing.
—Zephaniah 3:17

Emmy is my five-year-old granddaughter, and she is an only child. Her mom and dad have been trying to get her to sleep in her own room. The other night, her mom went in the room with her and lay down with her in her room. Laney read her a story and said prayers, and then she kissed her good-night. Laney started to leave the room, and Emmy wrapped herself around her mommy, saying, "Please don't leave me. I do not want to stay in my bed." Laney looked at Emmy and said, "Emmy, you cannot have a sleepover until you learn to sleep in your bed." With big tears in her eyes, she said to her mom, "Mom, do I look like I am ready for a sleepover?" Sometimes we want something, but we do not want to pay the cost. She will sleep in her bed, but that night was not the night.

Heidi's Farewell to Papa

And my tongue shall speak of Your righteousness
and of your Praise al the day long.
                                        —Psalm35:28 NKJV

A Farewell to Papa Ed

Good afternoon and thank you for coming to celebrate the life of Reverend Ed Rogers, better known to me as Papa Ed. My family and I are thankful for all you have done for us in the past few months. I had the privilege of having such an amazing person to call my Papa Ed. He loved many things, such as carpentry, taking photographs, traveling, being an inventor, and family. Most of all, he loved Jesus Christ. He was a pastor for thirty-six years, and I was his traveling buddy to his last church. I still wouldn't have my licenses if it wasn't for him. He would let me drive him to his last church. The family joked about him being prayed up enough to ride with me. I would have to say the thing I remember most on our drives is us talking about Jesus. He was not only my Papa Ed and my best friend but also my pastor. He was the main one that led me to Jesus, then baptized me.

A lot of you probably can relate to that. What he most wanted in life was to lead people to Jesus. One of his favorite verses was John3:16–17. Many people know John 3:16, but in my opinion, verse 17 is important as well (read John 3:16–17!). So in closing, I'd like to thank God for my precious Papa Ed. I will miss our early-morning phone calls as I would drive to work, and he would pray for me. The last time we talked on the phone, he prayed for me. He was the most selfless person I will ever meet. At this time, I'd like to challenge you. My Gega is speaking next, but please, if you don't know Jesus, accept Him. It would make Papa Ed happy to know he impacted even more lives after he was gone. My family and I will miss him dearly. However, we have peace knowing where he is. Now my Gega has something to share with you.

See You Later, My Precious Husband

Set your mind on things above,
not on things on the earth.
—Colossians 3:2 NKJV

My precious husband went to be with Jesus in February. He fought leukemia for 172 days, and the battle was tough. Ed and I shared forty-eight and a half years of marriage. We had five children of our own and helped foster four other children. We were blessed with five grandchildren. Ed accepted the call to preach thirty-three years ago and pastored several churches in North Carolina. He was an awesome man of God who loved deeply. This is the message I shared at his funeral:

To My Beloved Husband

Ed, thank you for forty-eight wonderful years of marriage. We were blessed with seven children: Marsha, Dawn, Tom, Tim, Jeff, and Susie and Heidi. Then God gave us Heidi, Dustin, Kassi, Tori, Cole, and Emmy, our wonderful grandchildren. Then God gave us a beautiful daughter and son through marriage. Ed, you were the smartest man I knew. Even more, you had the biggest heart. The children could ask any question, and you always knew the answers—

the right answer. They didn't ask me because they wanted the right answer. Your children said that they loved you, and this is what they said: Marsha, your smile; Dawn, your gentleness; Tom, your intelligence; Tim, your compassion for all. You accepted the call to the ministry. I went reluctantly unsure of this big adventure. A pastor's wife? Are you kidding?

We accepted the call and packed up our furniture and kids, not knowing what great adventure we would be on. There are no regrets. We were loved by the church families, most of them. You were a pastor. You could share the Word. You visited, prayed, and loved with all your heart. If they were hurting, you hurt. You always had time for all you met. You shared Jesus and lived Jesus. Cabbage-head dolls, overturned canoes, hikes in the woods, cutting wood (you also bought an old chicken house so you could teach the boys how to work)—your stories made life exciting, especially the field trip all the way to Colorado for a comic book. Wow, what a dad!

I knew my life with you would be whirlwind. We were married on Saturday at four o'clock, went to the Holiday Inn in Raleigh, got up on Sunday at five so we could be in church on Sunday. You described our marriage as a drag race. We packed ninety years' worth of life into forty-eight. The most wonderful blessings were that you loved the Lord with all your heart and wanted others to know of that love. You feed the homeless, the alcoholics, drug addict and all you met. Even in this horrible disease of leukemia, you served God well. You never complained, never asked God why, never told God what you had done for Him. Always, for all that was done to you, you answered with *thank you.* You believed in life, and you worked side by side with me in the Agape Pregnancy Center. You were my EPS: Ed positioning system. I always got lost when I went to speak at churches. I would call and ask, "Where am I?" and you would get me home.

I want to tell you couples today to enjoy every day together. Life ends so quickly. My dear sweet husband would say, "Don't talk about me tell. Them about Jesus." He wanted you to really live, and to live here and for eternity is to love Jesus and accept Him. Please make that decision for Christ today. Today is the day of salvation. Don't put off this decision.

Wednesday, Ed left this world and walked straight into the arms of Jesus. He is living, really living, now.

Our family wants to thank you for all you did for us during this difficult time. You prayed for us and sent donations to help us with our needs. I have loved Jesus since I was nine, but I really love Jesus now. He is a promise keeper, the lover of our soul, and he walks with us through the valleys.

Christians don't say goodbye. We say *see you later.*

My granddaughter said it best: "Papa Ed is with Jesus. I want to see him again."

My final decision is, I choose *joy.* I thank my Jesus for the wonderful years we had together. I will not pine over the ones we didn't have.

May God bless you all. I love you, and so did Ed.

Fifty Years of Prayer

Those who sow in tears Shall reap in joy. He who continually goes forth weeping, bearing seeds for sowing, Shall doubtless come again with rejoicing, Bringing his sheaves with him.
—Psalm 126:5–6 NKJV

Ed and I had been praying for a cousin for fifty years. We would ask about his salvation, and his answer was always, "I am almost there." Ed lay dying with leukemia, and he asked Roy to come see him. Roy and his wife came. Once again we asked about his relationship with Jesus, and once again his answer was, "I am almost there." I told him that almost is not enough and would not get him into heaven. Then Ed led Roy in the salvation prayer. We praised God that he had accepted Jesus. After Ed died, I was invited to Roy's baptism. I know that Ed was rejoicing in heaven with all the angels.

We should never give up on the ones we love. Continue to pray and continue to ask if they know Jesus. We had another friend come to the home when Ed was sick. He had prayed for this man for many years also. All this man could do was cry; he said he loved Ed so much. I asked him if he had accepted Jesus. His answer was, "I don't want to talk about it now." I told him when he left that because of his decision, he would never see Ed again. Two men, each with a decision, one chose Jesus; the other one is running. We can pray, but the decision is always theirs. I continue to pray for the second person. Don't give up.

The Candle Blew Out

Arise, shine for your light has come!
—Isaiah 60:1 NKJV

Ed was in the hospital for many days. I would come home to get clean clothes and check on things at the home and run the pregnancy ministry. One night I came in and went to the ministry. I washed clothes, cleaned the house, checked on things, and I noticed that one of the electric candles had blown out. I have six candles in my windows to represent my family. I saw the burned-out candle, and I cried. That was Ed's candle, and I knew that Jesus was coming to take him home.

As the time drew closer for Ed to leave us, he would ask to sit up in the bed so he could talk to Jesus. His last day with us, he talked about the gold floor, and he told me he had to be there for the roll call. Ten minutes later, he was there for the roll call. You see, Ed's light in this world went out, but his eternal light with Jesus will burn forever. God's promises are true. Jesus came to Ed and told him of His love for him and that all the things he had read and preached from the Word were true. Make sure your light is shining for Jesus.

Debt Paid

Those who sow in tears shall reap in joy.
—Psalm 126:5 NKJV

We prepared for Ed's funeral. The medical bills were staggering, the income was limited, and now we had to figure out a way to pay for a funeral. The funeral, even a simple one, cost $12,500, and that was not opening the casket or using the funeral home for the viewing. My daughter borrowed some money, and I prayed that God would help us. Good friends of ours that we had known for a long time called us and paid for the entire funeral bill. It was a blessing. Then the collection agencies started calling for the medical bills to be paid. There was no estate, no insurance, no savings—I was not sure how I was going to pay all of this.

Ed had attended Antioch Baptist Church as a child. He was ordained there, and we called it our home church. They called, and they wanted to do a BBQ benefit to help with the medical bills. The whole church came together, and men cooked BBQ all night; the ladies packed the meat and made homemade desserts to sell. Many people purchased bags of BBQ. Some of the churches that Ed had pastored sent love offerings. The benefit netted over $12,000, and this paid off all the medical bills. We serve a mighty God, and God's people are wonderful. I thank God for all these precious saints and ask a blessing on each and every one of them.

Robbery to Blessing

Restore to me the joy of my salvation, and
uphold me with by your generous Spirit.
—Psalm 51:12 (NKJV)

The Agape Pregnancy Center has lots of supplies for babies coming in, so we purchased large storage bins to put outside the building with locks. We had gotten a large amount of diapers, wipes, and receiving blankets, so we stored them in the bins until we were ready for them. I came to the center after a weekend and found that someone had cut the locks and stolen all the baby supplies. Why would anyone want all those blankets, diapers, and wipes? We called the police and reported the thief. The amount stolen was over $4,500 worth. I started praying for the thieves. The police said they would probably sell the baby items on the street for drugs. I asked God to replace what the devil had stolen from the center, and before the night was over, he did. One church had made lots of beautiful handmade blankets for the babies, another church had a diaper and wipes drive, and there were so many boxes of diapers. God replaced all that was stolen and more. God is the winner, not the enemy.

Mount Diaper

Bring ye all the tithes into the storehouse, that there may be meat in mine house and try me now.
—Malachi 3:10 NKJV

Part of my job as a director of a life ministry is to speak at churches and civic groups and share about the crisis pregnancy ministry. On Sunday, I spoke at a church in the morning and went to a baby shower at a different church that afternoon. I drove my daughter's car that Sunday, and God blessed us with an awesome baby shower. The car was packed, and I praised God for all the baby items that would take care of our precious little ones. Just as I was getting in my car, an elderly lady came up and gave me $30 cash and told me to buy some diapers for the babies. I thanked her and put the money in the center bag. I remembered that there was a drugstore that was changing companies, and I was going to check the next day to see if there were any diapers on sale. God spoke to me. He said, *We are going to get the diapers today.*

I was not sure if I knew where the drugstore was. I imagined that the manager would think I was crazy asking for diapers. God reminded me that you have not because you ask not. I walked into the store and found the manager. I told him that I was a director of a crisis pregnancy center, and I needed diapers for the babies. I showed him the $30 and asked how many diapers could I get for that amount. The tall man started crying, and I thought I must have hurt his feelings. You see, this manager was a Christian. He had been in his storage room where there were rows of diapers that were not his brand. He had just prayed, "Lord, what am I going to do with all these diapers?" He looked at me and told me to stand there; he would be right back. He came back with a huge case of diapers. He smiled, and I tried to give him the money. He said, "Lady, I am not finished yet." I stood there in amazement. The manager came back with eleven more huge cases of diapers. I knew that God performed the miracle of the fish and loaves. I counted the diapers, and there were 3,300 diapers. I asked him, "How much do I owe you for the diapers.?" He smiled and said, "That will be $30 cash and no tax!" He smiled and walked away singing. I looked in amazement at the awesome God we serve and how God even cares for the little babies' behinds.

People walked by me and stared at this mountain of diapers. What was a fifty-year-old woman going to do with so many diapers? How was I going to get the diapers to the center? My little car was full of the baby-shower items. I simply said, "God are you still there?" He replied, *Helen, I said I would never leave you nor forsake you. I have someone coming to take the diapers to the center. Just stand here. She will be here in ten minutes.*

In about ten minutes, a teacher friend of mine that I had not seen in two years showed up. She told me she had been asleep on the couch, and God had woken her up and told her to come and find Helen at the drugstore. She looked at me, and then she looked at the mountain of diapers and said, "What is that?" I asked her my question first, "What are you driving?" She told me she had her van. I said that was good because God had sent her to help me get all these diapers to the center. She did, and many babies were blessed because of an awesome and mighty God who meets every need in our lives. I learned that when God asks you to do something, He has a plan and a blessing. God had a divine appointment for the manager and me to meet that day. Two prayers were answered and many babies blessed.

Bucket of Blessings

And we know that all things work together for good
to them who are called according to His purpose.
—Romans 8:28 NKJV

I have been working in crisis pregnancy centers for thirty-four years. This ministry has taught me to walk entirely in faith. All of our funding to keep the doors open comes from Christian people and churches who love God and life.

This miracle shows the creativity and humor of the God we serve. The rent was due for the center by Monday, and it was Friday. I checked the bank account, and we had $200 in the bank. But the rent was $700. God has taught me over the years to thank Him for meeting our needs before we see them.

My prayer that morning was a thank-you to God for providing the rent. I also prayed that God would send the money creatively. You see, I knew God could send a check for the amount, but I like seeing the creative side of God. I went to school and placed my cell phone on my desk. The phone rang, and it was a man named Ray. Ray said he had a donation for the center and would my husband and I meet him at Hardee's at six that evening. He said he would need my husband to help with the donation since it was so heavy. I wondered if the donation was baby furniture. I called Ed, and we met Ray at Hardee's at 6:00 p.m. He drove up in a handyman van. He called my husband over, and they placed a ten-gallon bucket in my van. I thought, *What could possibly be in that container?* Ray took the lid off, and the bucket was full of quarters. I smiled and asked

God how much was in the bucket. He said, *I would have to count it to find out!*

Ray told me he had been saving the quarters for a year. In Ray's devotion that morning, God told him to call me and to get the bucket of change to me today because it was needed. Guess how much money was in the bucket? God had sent $601 in a ten-gallon bucket to pay for the rent at the center. He had done creatively. I learned that my God has many ways to answer prayers. God is so unique and not limited as we are.

From Death to Life

For His anger endureth but a moment; in
His favour is life; weeping endures for a
night, but joy comes in the morning.
—Psalm 30:5 NKJV

My husband and I have been involved in starting crisis pregnancy centers in several counties in North Carolina. Ed was a pastor, and we felt the call to come to Fayetteville, North Carolina. We started the Agape Pregnancy Support Services in a house on Cedar Creek Road. After we had been there for two years, something happened to change our location. Fayetteville was the home of an abortion clinic that had been there for twenty-seven years. Many thousands of babies died in that clinic. Many Christians in that community would drive by the clinic and pray that the doors would close. God did answer their prayers, and the doors closed. The building was abandoned, and the homeless broke into the building and stayed at night.

One night I was restless, and so I decided to read a book called *The Dream Giver* by Dr. Bruce Wilkerson. In this book, the author talks about getting out of our comfort zones and walking by faith. The next morning, God asked me to get out of my comfort zone and go purchase the old abortion building. I told God that I didn't want that old building—didn't He have a new building somewhere? I said, "Lord, this is a place of death." God said, *I have a special plan for this place. I am going to take back what Satan has used for evil and death and redeem it. I will bring life to this place and honor to Me.* The price was $120,000. I reminded God I was a kindergarten teacher, and I didn't have 120 cents. I knew God would have to provide the money.

God promised if we walk by faith, we would see miracles. Ed and I went into the old building; it was a disgusting mess. It was filled with drug needles, wine and beer bottles, old clothes, feces, and condoms where the homeless had stayed.

The windows were boarded up, and it was very dark. We walked into the building carrying flashlights. You could feel the evil in the place. Each room had a plan, and God spoke its future use. At the back of the building, there were two procedure rooms with Formica walls and drains in the floor to wash out the blood from the abortions. One procedure room had equipment left in there with blood on the machine and blood on the wall. I stood at the door feeling like I was going to throw up. God said, *You have to go in the room. You must feel what I feel.* As I walked into the room, I could feel death, pain, and so much sorrow and regrets. I heard the babies crying because they did not get to fulfill God's plan for their life. I heard the mothers weeping because they had killed their children. The third voice in that room was my Lord and Savior weeping for all that was lost.

I answered with a *yes*, I would work the ministry from this location. He reminded me that it would cost greatly. The answer was still yes! One month later, my mom died. God revealed that the two procedure rooms would be a chapel and an ultrasound room. The chapel would be a place for women to come and find the forgiveness for their abortions. It would be a place to come out of the darkness and come into the light of Jesus. A man in our church did purchase the building, and we make payments to him each month with no interest. We started working on the building, and we anointed each room. We prayed, painted, and cleaned all for the glory of Jesus.

The first room to get the boards off the windows was the chapel. As the boards came down, the light of Jesus flooded the building. You could feel that Jesus had reclaimed what the enemy had for a season. I told my husband, "Look, honey, there goes the devil with his bags packed, and he will not be coming back to this place."

The Agape Pregnancy Support Services is on the rough side of town. We have prostitutes, drug addicts, pimps, and the homeless walking the streets in front of the building. I had a dear Christian lady ask me if I knew what kind of people were on that side of town.

I smiled and said, "Yes, I do. I am exactly where Jesus would be." We know that God has placed us at this place for such a time as this. We are able to minister to the people of the streets and our clients. I see God taking people from death to life eternally just as He did with this old abortion clinic. God is the author of life both physically and eternally.

Paid in Full

*Bear ye one another burdens and
so fulfill the law of Christ.*
—Galatians 6:2 NKJV

My dear precious husband passed away on February 20, 2019. We battled through 172 days of leukemia. It was horrible, but my precious husband kept the faith, never blaming God and always trusting Him. My husband was a Baptist pastor for thirty-four years and served God faithfully. He served in six different churches during this time. He preached the Word faithfully every Sunday. He baptized people; he performed funerals and visited the shut-ins and the ones in the hospital. He impacted many people's lives for the good.

When Ed died, we were without funds to bury him. We had spent most of what we had at the three hospital stays during this time. I went to the funeral home; I tried to cut cost. We would use his home church for the viewing and burial. I asked how much the funeral was. The director said, "That is $12,500." He wanted the money before the funeral the next day. I prayed and tried to think of ways to get the money. Ed had a friend and deacon whom he had traveled across the United States with so Ed could take photographs. They had remained true friends even when Ed left that church. I got a call from the funeral home that the bill was paid in full. The friend had paid the bill. God had performed another miracle. I stopped by to thank them. He said God had told him to pay the bill. God always answers prayers. Sometimes now, sometimes later, and sometimes the answer is not what you had prayed for.

The Dream

*Then saidth he unto his disciples, the harvest
truly is plenteous, but the laborers are few.*
—Matthew 9:37 NKJV

I grew up on a farm, and Daddy grew acres of cotton. I would stand in the middle of the cotton field holding Daddy's hand. If you looked at the sky, you could see that there was a terrible storm coming. The cotton needed to be picked before the storm came. I said, "Daddy, how are we ever going to get all the cotton in before the storm comes?" Daddy smiled and said, "Helen, God will provide."

We looked up and saw all the relatives and neighbors coming down the road bringing their cotton sacks (there were no big cotton-picking machines back in those days). Everyone worked hard and picked all day. Soon the harvest was safe from the storms. All the friends and relatives put the food they had brought together, and we had a feast. My cousins and I would play games, one of them was called "there ain't no booger bears out tonight, Daddy killed them all last night."

We would run and chase lightning bugs and put them in mason jars. They made great night-lights. Everyone went home, and the storms came. I was safe in my bed with the lightning bugs flickering. The thunder was loud, and the lightning flashed, and the hard rains came. As I lay there in my bed, safe and dry, I could hear my Daddy's words ringing in my ears, "God will provide, Helen!" God did provide, and He still provides for us every day.

The other night, I saw the cotton fields ripe unto harvest. Each cotton bowl was the face of a precious baby waiting to be born. On the horizon is abortion led by the devil himself. He is coming to kill and steal. There are a few workers in the field with spectators on the sidelines. The spectators are shouting, "Save the babies!" The spectators will not leave the sidelines to help. I stand in the middle of the cotton field crying for all the precious babies that would lose their lives because Christians did nothing. For babies to die from abortion, all it takes is Christian people doing nothing. I woke up in tears. Will you help fight the battle? God will provide, and you are the answer.

The Nightmare

For I did not come to call the righteous,
but sinners to repentance.
—Matthew 9:13 NKJV

I speak at many churches and groups about the pregnancy ministries. In all these years, I have never met a woman who was glad she had an abortion.

Not so long ago, I met an eighty-one-year-old woman who had nine children, lots of grandchildren, and great-grandchildren. Her life was full of family, but she had a dark secret she had never shared. When she was sixteen, she got pregnant out of wedlock. Her family obtained a secret abortion for her so that no one would know. She knew, and it was etched in her heart forever. She told me of the nights she cried for the child she had killed. Her nights were filled with the cries of her aborted child. She had many more children, but there was still a missing piece in her heart. In this pregnancy ministry, we call the women who have had abortions the *walking wounded*. This woman finally accepted the forgiveness from God and has forgiven herself. God is the only one who can heal the broken hearts of the women who have had abortions. Once the truth comes to light, the devil has no more hold over you.

Is there something in your life you have hidden and you are in need of healing? Give it to Jesus!

Jesus with Skin On

But the path of the just is as the shinning sun,
that shines even brighter unto the perfect day.
—Proverbs 4:18 NKJV

I was pregnant, scared, and alone, and you gossiped about me and discussed my predicament. I was kicked out of my home when my parents found out I was pregnant. You looked away and said I could get welfare. I had no clothes for my new baby. You said I was an unfit mother. I wanted to give my baby life, but there was no one to show me how. I was lonely, and you turned your back on me and pointed out my sins. I needed Jesus, and you were afraid to tell me about Him. You seem so close to God, but I'm still pregnant, scared, and alone! What will I do? I feel so trapped. I wanted more for my baby that I had. Does anyone care? I will care with God's love. I will love you, pray for you, and help you. I have clothes for your baby. I will mentor you and teach you how to be a good mom. Most of all, I would like to introduce you to Jesus. You see, Jesus loves you and your baby. He has plans for you both. I will be the hands, the feet, and the heart of Jesus. I will be Jesus with skin on. Jesus is your only hope.

Deeper

Thomas Rogers

*But I have trusted in thy mercy; my heart shall
rejoice in thy salvation. I will sing unto the Lord,
because he hath dealt bountifully with me.*
—Psalm 13:5–6 NKJV

Deeper and Deeper
Deeper and Deeper, Lord
I want to go.
Deeper and Deeper, Lord
Into Thy grace.
Deeper and Deeper, Lord
Let Thy love flow.
Deeper and Deeper, Lord
Till I see thy face.
So let the praises ring
Deeper and Deeper.
To the Immortal Kind
Deeper and Deeper
Till the songs of angels sink
Deeper and Deeper
Into the hearts of men.
Deeper and Deeper
Until they glory Him without end.

A Gate to Heaven

Thomas Rogers

*I called upon your name, O LORD, out of the
lowest pit. You have heard my voice, do not
hide your ear at my breathing, at my cry.
Fear not O Lord, thou hast pleaded the causes
of my soul, thou hast redeemed my life.*
                              —Lamentations 3:55–56 NKJV

Here is the quietness of this time
Nothing but the sound of a beating broken heart
And the quiet but steady race of pulse
Nervously awaiting a meeting
With a King.
Humbly bowed down on weak knees,
The head hung lowly in its place,
With a clasp of hands,
Slowly I begin to pray
Without a doubt in mind
Waiting for a reply…
All of a sudden
As quick as the wind
And just as soft
Comes
"I am with you, child."
A shock shudders my very soul
As I feel the presence of the Holy One.

My heart races
As His presences falls upon me.
My faith is reassured
For God's Son
Has opened a door
A gate to Heaven.

Deep Waters

Thomas Rogers

He reached down from on high and
took hold of me out of deep waters.
                    —2 Samuel 22:18 NKJV

I was splashing around
In the sea of this world,
I screamed and screamed
Yet no one answers my call
Sinking,
Weighted down by sin,
Drowning
In my own evil doings,
Gasping,
A sin chokes my soul,
With No other hope
I begin to pray;
A prayer of pleading for
Help!
Wait, has someone grabbed me
Hand?
I am gently lifted
From the sea
Taken to higher ground
A place
Called
Heaven!

Saved from the stormy waters of life
By Christ
The Prince of Peace
My Lord, my Savior
My Friend!

Heart Ablaze
Thomas Rogers

For it is the God who commanded light to shine
out of darkness who has shone in our hearts.
—2 Corinthians 4:6 NKJV

When there comes the darkness of sin,
It falls like night, darkening us within.
It extinguishes our souls' eternal flame,
Yet our hope lies in only one name,
And that name is JESUS, Our Friend.
He lights a new fire and extinguishes sin,
He recreates the eternal flame anew,
Lighting the heart ablaze inside you.
So, O children of God, let us sing,
To God, Who sends out hope on angel wings.
Doors
Life is a hallway filled with doors,
One on every side and every floor.
There are so many ways to choose,
With some you win, with some you lose,
But with many choices,
Which way to go?
That is what we all need to know.
All the doors seem to lead to misery,
And it seems as though there's no good to see,
But just when life is getting you down,
There is one good door yet to be found.

And that door is the door of peace,
Upon opening it your joy will increase,
Because behind this door is a Friend,
Giving you LIFE that never ends—JESUS!

Active Child

Thomas Rogers

Behold, children are a heritage from the Lord,
and the fruit of the womb is his reward.
—Psalm 127:3

Kicking, running, swimming,
I do it all day,
I am so very active,
In both life and play.
My ears can hear sound,
My tongue can taste the salt,
My eyes still see darkness,
But my senses bear no faults.
My heart beats soundly,
My brain waves are there,
My lungs are preparing,
To breathe a world of air.
The One who made me,
Formed the very earth,
He loved me so much.
He knew me before birth.
Yet one day came,
When my home was invaded,
By a loud vacuum
I felt so violated.
Then the horror came
As I was being torn apart,

Then these words came,
As my soul began to depart,
"This is really the right thing,
The best thing to do,
You are saving your child
From a bad life with you."
Then I saw my body,
As my spirit left the womb,
I saw my mom in tears,
As a voice called me from the tomb.
And now I stay in heaven,
Where there is no sin or strife,
But I am left to wander,
How could my Mother take my life?

Best Gift

For God so loved the world, that he gave his only
begotten Son, that whosoever believeth in him
should not perish, but have everlasting life.
—John 3:16 KJV

Tori, one of my six-year-old granddaughters, was sitting outside under our one-hundred-year-old oak tree with me. As we were sitting outside enjoying the beautiful spring weather, we started to talk about God's creation. As we talked, Tori looked at me with her big blue eyes and said, "Gega, I love you so much!" I told her that I loved her too and that she is my sunshine. Tori loves to sing, so we sang "You Are My Sunshine." Tori sang a little better than I did. As the song ended, Tori looked at me and said, "I really love Jesus. I need to ask Jesus into my heart." I helped lead her in prayer to ask for forgiveness and to ask Jesus into her heart. That beautiful spring day, God gave me the greatest gift: my precious Tori became a Christian. I pray for all my grandchildren, and this was one of the greatest highlights of my life—to lead Tori in prayer. I believe God has awesome plans for Tori and for all of them. Tori is compassionate and loving and strong-willed. I know God can use all these traits for His service. Thank You, God, for the gift of salvation!

About the Author

Helen McLeod Rogers lives in Lillington, North Carolina. She was married to Reverend Ed Rogers for forty-eight and a half years. Her precious husband went to heaven on February 20, 2019. They have six living children and five precious grandchildren. Helen has a master's degree in early childhood and has taught kindergarten for forty years in North Carolina.

Thirty-two years ago, Helen took a stand for *life*. Since that time, Ed and Helen have started several pregnancy centers in North Carolina. At the present, Helen is the director of the Agape Pregnancy Support Services in Fayetteville, North Carolina, with outreaches in Harnett and Robeson Counties. Over the years, they have seen over forty thousand babies saved from abortion. Helen calls them her *god children*. Helen's first book is titled *God Loves You Better Than Mac and Cheese*. The second book is titled *That's Such a God Thing*. This third book is ordained by God.